On the Map

Mapping History

Cynthia Kennedy Henzel

ABDO
Publishing Company

visit us at
www.abdopublishing.com

Published by ABDO Publishing Company, 8000 West 78th Street, Edina, Minnesota 55439.
Copyright © 2008 by Abdo Consulting Group, Inc. International copyrights reserved in all
countries. No part of this book may be reproduced in any form without written permission from the
publisher. The Checkerboard Library™ is a trademark and logo of ABDO Publishing Company.

Printed in the United States.

Cover Photo: AP Images
Interior Photos: Alamy p. 19; AP Images pp. 5, 9, 10, 11; Corbis p. 17; Getty Images pp. 15, 23;
     iStockphoto pp. 8, 20; Library of Congress pp. 25, 27; National Geographic Image Collection
     p. 7; North Wind pp. 6, 13, 14, 22; Photo Researchers pp. 21, 24, 26

Series Coordinator: BreAnn Rumsch
Editors: Rochelle Baltzer, BreAnn Rumsch
Art Direction & Cover Design: Neil Klinepier

Library of Congress Cataloging-in-Publication Data

Henzel, Cynthia Kennedy, 1954-
  Mapping history / Cynthia Kennedy Henzel.
      p. cm. -- (On the map)
  Includes bibliographical references and index.
  ISBN 978-1-59928-951-9
  1. Cartography--History--Juvenile literature. I. Title.

  GA105.6.H475 2008
  526.09--dc22

                              2007029202

Contents

Ancient Maps

Maps show us the places we want to learn about and how to get to them. Even ancient peoples needed to know where to find fresh water and the best hunting grounds. The earliest maps were probably scratched in sand. So, we will never know who drew the first map.

But, there are many examples of ancient maps from around the world. Eskimos carved maps into bone. The Incas of South America built maps from stone. In the South Pacific, Marshall Islanders made stick maps of ocean currents so the fishers could guide their boats. In Turkey, a **mural** painted more than 8,000 years ago shows houses and a volcano.

Identifying the oldest map is difficult because not everyone agrees what a map is. A carving on a mammoth tusk from Ukraine shows houses along a river. It is more than 12,000 years old! Is this the oldest map? Or, is it just a picture of houses?

Scientists and historians study ancient maps to understand how our world was discovered. Today, many of these maps are extremely valuable or even priceless.

Maps have always displayed information as a picture. Today, we commonly think of maps as a way to illustrate measurements about a place. These measurements include distance, direction, relative size, and other information.

Mapping Civilizations

Several nations made up ancient Mesopotamia, which was just north of the Arabian Peninsula.

Historians trace the first modern maps to the ancient land of Mesopotamia. This area is in modern-day Iraq. Great civilizations flourished there, where the Euphrates and Tigris rivers flow through the desert. Farmers lived along the rivers. They used the river water to irrigate their land.

The Mesopotamian rulers taxed their people's crops and livestock. They used this tax to build irrigation canals and great cities, as well as to maintain armies. Maps were made to show each farm's boundaries. This told the rulers how much tax each farmer owed.

One map found in Mesopotamia is believed to be the oldest discovered so far. The map was made about 4,500 years ago by Babylonians. Babylon was one of the civilizations in Mesopotamia. The map was scratched on a small clay tablet. It is small enough to fit in the palm of your hand!

Some ancient Mesopotamian tablets show mountains and farmland. Others feature cuneiform, one of the earliest alphabet systems.

The map shows the boundaries of about 30 acres (12 ha) of land that belonged to a person named Azala. It has many features that are also found on modern maps. For example, directions are labeled. Circles show the locations of nearby towns. And, a line through the center represents a river.

Improving Accuracy

Another great civilization began west of Mesopotamia in Egypt. The Nile River provided water to Egyptian farmers. But the Nile flooded each year, washing away boundary markers between the farms. However, the Egyptians used **geometry** to measure their farmland and make maps. After the floods, they used the maps to replace the lost markers.

One of the oldest surviving Egyptian maps is about 3,000 years old. The map is drawn on papyrus, which is a type of paper made from water reeds. It is kept in a museum in Turin, Italy. So, the map is sometimes called the Turin Papyrus.

Papyrus is plentiful in Egypt.

The Turin Papyrus is much more **accurate** than most early maps. It shows the relative size of different areas and accurate distances between places. The map also shows the various types of rocks with different colored dots. Areas where rock and gold could be mined are marked. These features make the papyrus the first **geologic** map.

Papyrus often served more than one purpose. While one side might show a map, the back could contain written records or artwork. When these rolls are discovered, they must be carefully unrolled to preserve these features.

Greek Advancements

The next great step in mapmaking came from the Greeks about 2,500 years ago. Until this time, most people believed the earth was flat.

In the 500s BC, Greek mathematician Pythagoras (puh-THAG-uh-ruhs) noticed that the height of the stars changed at different locations. He also noticed that when a ship sailed toward land, the masts appeared before the rest of the ship. So, he concluded that the earth was a **sphere**. But, not everyone was convinced.

In the 300s BC, Greek philosopher and scientist Aristotle used scientific observation and proved Pythagoras right. One night, he observed a **lunar eclipse** cast the earth's shadow onto the moon. Aristotle realized that this shadow was always curved.

During a lunar eclipse, the moon acts like a mirror for Earth's curved shadow.

Today, satellite imaging shows accurate data of the planet's shape and surface.

Since a **sphere** always has a curved shadow, he reasoned that the earth must be a sphere.

During the 200s BC, Greek mathematician Eratosthenes (ehr-uh-TAHS-thuh-neez) made two major contributions to mapmaking. First, he used mathematics to calculate the distance around the earth. He accomplished this by measuring angles formed by the sun's rays as they hit the earth. This way, he never had to leave home to make his calculations!

Eratosthenes also developed a system of **horizontal** and **vertical** lines called a grid to find places on a map. A grid system works much like putting a piece of clear graph paper over a map. Points on the grid make finding places on the map much easier.

In 146 BC, the Romans conquered Greece. They also conquered the ancient lands of Mesopotamia, Egypt, southern Europe, and England. By 44 BC, the Romans had conquered all of Italy and created the vast Roman Empire.

As a result, the work of Greek scholars was introduced in Rome. Greek geographer Strabo lived in Rome during this time. About AD 23, he recorded the Greek discoveries in his book *Geography*. His book includes the only lasting record of Eratosthenes's world map.

But, *Geography* only describes part of the earth. Strabo thought lands north of England were too cold for people to live. And, he believed everywhere below Egypt was too hot. Strabo did not think it was important to have an **accurate** grid system for the entire earth. That is because he thought people lived in such a small area.

The modern world is hard to recognize on Eratosthenes's map. Finding Europe helps orient the rest of the map.

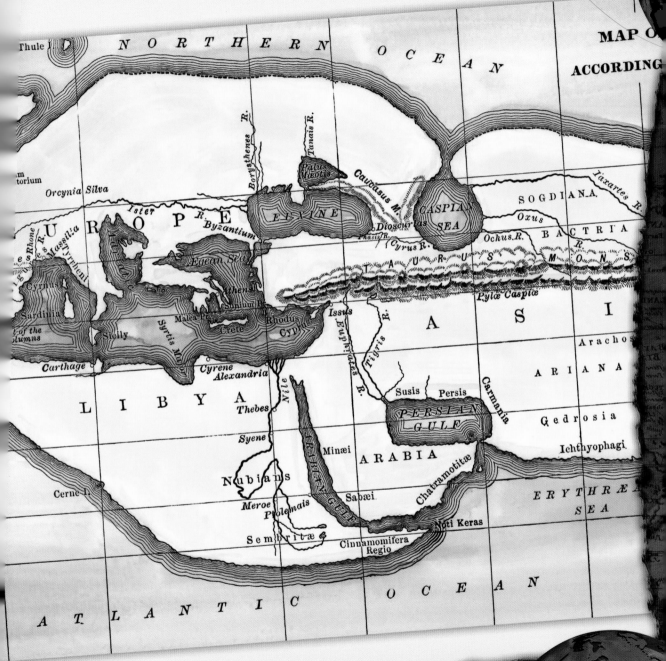

Thule I.

N O R T H E R N   O C E A N

...m
...torium

Orcynia Silva

Borysthenes R.

Tanais R.

Palus Mæotis

Caucasus M.

E U R O P E

Ister

Massilia

Rhone

Byzantium

EUXINE

Dioscurias

Phasis R.   Cyrus R.

CASPIAN SEA

SOGDIANA

Iaxartes R.

Oxus

Ochus R.

BACTRIA

MONS

Tyrrheni

Egean Sea

T   A   U   R   U   S

Cyrnus

Athens

Sunium P.

Pylæ Caspiæ

A   S   I

Sardinia

Malea Pr.

Crete

Rhodus

Cyprus

Issus

Euphrates R.

Tigris R.

Arachos

...of the
...lumns

Sicily

Syrtis Mag.

Cyprus

ARIANA

Carthage

Cyrene
Alexandria

Thebes

Nile

Susis

Persis

Carmania

Gedrosia

L   I   B   Y   A

Syene

PERSIAN GULF

Ichthyophagi

Minæi

ARABIA

Cerne I.

Nubians

Chatramotitæ

E   R   Y   T   H   R   Æ
S   E   A

Meroe

Ptolemais

Sabæi

Noti Keras

Sembritæ

Cinnamomifera
Regio

A   T   L   A   N   T   I   C   O   C   E   A   N

Ptolemy

Ptolemy

Sometime after the year AD 150, Egyptian geographer Ptolemy (TAHL-uh-mee) determined that a grid system was necessary to create **accurate** maps. At this time, most maps were copied by hand from other maps. Ptolemy felt this method left too much room for error. After all, one tiny copying mistake could move a river many miles!

Ptolemy believed mathematical **coordinates** would help mapmakers put places in exactly the same spots. So, he developed a new grid system. Ptolemy carefully measured the coordinates of many places for his book *Geographia*.

Many places did not have prior data for these measurements. So, Ptolemy estimated those locations based on reports about the direction and the time travelers took to get somewhere.

Also, Ptolemy did not use Eratosthenes's **accurate** measure of the distance around the earth. He thought the earth was smaller. As a result, known places such as the Mediterranean Sea were stretched over too many degrees of longitude. And, the unknown world was too small.

This was an important mistake. Later explorers sailing west to reach Asia used Ptolemy's map. As a result, they believed the distance they would travel was much less than it really was.

Ptolemy used several modern techniques to create his map. Yet, it looks much different than the world atlases we see today. Can you pick out any familiar places?

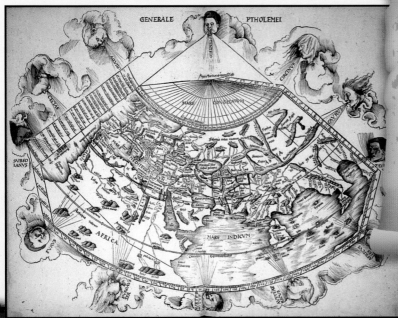

Ptolemy's Grid

Ptolemy created the grid system that came to be known as latitude and longitude. He made the equator the starting point for his grid. He added lines of longitude that ran north and south. Then, he drew lines of latitude that were parallel with the equator.

Ptolemy named these lines by the length of the longest day at that distance from the equator. In other words, each line was labeled in hours and minutes. Ptolemy's system was similar to the modern latitude and longitude system. But today, we measure both lines of latitude and longitude in degrees.

15

A Biblical Interpretation

The Middle Ages began with the fall of the Roman Empire in AD 476. This period lasted hundreds of years. The great centers of learning in Greece, Rome, and Egypt were destroyed by war. And, books and libraries were burned. Much of the knowledge discovered by Greeks and Romans was lost during the early years of this period.

During the Middle Ages, the most educated Europeans were Christian monks. They believed that all knowledge came from reading the Bible. And, they were not interested in observations or mathematics like the Greeks.

So, the monks drew their maps based on biblical information. Many of them believed the Bible said the world was flat like a coin. The monks created maps for pilgrims traveling to holy places. They put biblical places, such as the Garden of Eden, on these maps.

FUN FACT

Many maps from this period included mythical creatures, such as sea monsters and dragons. These images added decoration to areas that were still unexplored.

The most common type of map from the Middle Ages is called a T and O map. The top of the map pointed east. Jerusalem, the most holy place, was in the center. A *T* divided the map into three parts. The top half was Asia. On the bottom half, the vertical line of the *T* divided Europe and Africa. The *O* represented the ocean that surrounded these lands.

Muslim Influence

Not all Greek knowledge was lost during the Middle Ages. Arab scholars translated the work of Ptolemy into Arabic. During the AD 800s, **Muslim** mathematician al-Khwarizmi (al-KWAHR-ihz-mee) improved the **accuracy** of Ptolemy's world map. He added measurements from the Islamic lands of the Middle East and northern Africa.

Another Islamic scholar, al-Biruni (al-bee-ROO-nee), wrote *Cartography* in 995. He studied how to use **projections**. This is the method of making flat maps accurate when depicting the round Earth. He also took many measurements and calculated an accurate distance around the earth.

The **cartographer** al-Idrisi (uhl-ih-DREE-see) also made important contributions to mapmaking. He traveled and combined new and old knowledge of the world onto a map. This was the most complete map of the world during the 1100s.

By the end of the Middle Ages, the knowledge of the Greeks was lost in Europe. But, it was preserved and expanded in Islamic lands.

N.

Burtenea
Felowia.
Afransheah.
DenmarK.
Germania.
Jenubea.
Bejeerat.
Asiatic
Ruſſia.
Yajooj.
al-Mutensh.
Hurab.
al-Alman
TurKesh.
Majooj.
AsKush.
TaKhernea.
Italia.
Mukhaldanach
Izzea.
Kulhoa.
Keimak.
Corsa
Sardinia.
Albeian.
TurKea.
al-Khuzzus.
Kurjeea.
al-Shash.
al-Nufus.
AbreeKea.
Azerbijan.
Chuwarizm
al-Sefur.
al-Sousnea.
al-Hureed.
Seharee
Berenech.
al-Beharis.
al-Tribut.
Belad
Nemaneh.
al-Multa
u Sinhajeh.
al-Irak
Khorasan.
al-Seen.
Curan.
Miſsur.
al-Sham.
Fars.
al-Fazeh.
Canum.
Kirman.
al-Kind.
Negroland.
Gowas.
Mugham.
al-Sunda.
Belad Musrata.
Afouahat.
al-Saueed.
al-Saueed.
al-Dau.
Comr.
Belad al-Lemlun.
al-Hejus.
al-Beja.
al-Shujur.
Ceylon.
Thiamu.
al-Yemen.
al-Taideen.
al-Nuba.
al-Habesh.
al Wak Wak.
Lacs
et Sources
du Nil.
Berbera.
al-Zuag.
Sefala.

Montagnes de la Lune.

Islamic world maps are centered on the Middle East. While they give a general picture of the world, they are based on points of latitude and longitude.

AMERICA

Chinese Exploration

Cheng Ho traveled on ships called junks. His ships were built to hold many treasures. So, they were much larger than modern junks. They were also swift vessels that could navigate both rivers and the open seas.

While the Greeks were busy mapping the West, the Chinese were mapping the East. Maps were important in both places for the same reasons. Farmers along great rivers needed to know the boundaries of their land. Traders needed to know travel routes. And, generals had to know where to send their armies.

Then during the **Ming dynasty**, a great Chinese admiral named Cheng Ho (JUHNG-HOH) began his explorations. Cheng Ho grew up in southwestern China. But he was **Muslim**, and his family had traveled in the West.

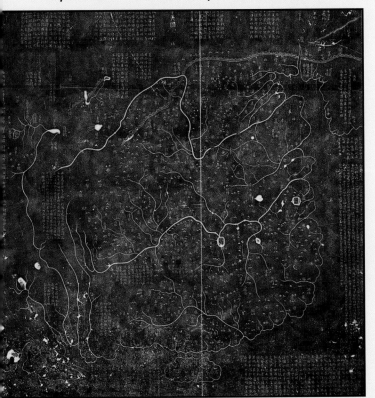

Maps created on stone are unique to Chinese tradition.

Cheng Ho's great treasure **fleet** explored new lands for gold, ivory, and other treasures. Between 1405 and 1435, he sailed as far west as Mozambique and Egypt. Some historians believe he explored as far east as California. This was more than 50 years before Christopher Columbus's voyage to the **New World**!

Cheng Ho brought new information about the world to China. This helped mapmakers create more **accurate** maps. But eventually, the government thought exploring new places was unimportant. They would not give more money to the treasure fleet. So for China, exploration of the world ceased.

The Age of Exploration

In Europe, the Age of Exploration was just beginning. European scholars translated Ptolemy's *Geographia* into Latin in about 1405. **Muslims** had used Ptolemy's work to advance mapmaking. Now Europeans would use it, too.

Henry the Navigator

Europeans wanted to find new routes to Asia. Like the Chinese, they wanted to trade and discover treasures. But, it was expensive and risky to travel east by land. Great deserts blocked the paths, and bandits roamed the roads. Europeans needed to find a way to sail east.

In Portugal, Prince Henry the Navigator led

the way. Beginning in 1420, his crews sailed south along Africa's west coast. Each voyage brought new discoveries. In 1457, the Portuguese hired an Italian monk named Brother Mauro to make a new world map. This map recorded the Portuguese discoveries.

Finally, Portuguese explorer Bartolomeu Dias set out to discover a route around Africa. In 1488, he sailed around the southern tip of the continent. Today, this location is known as the Cape of Good Hope.

Brother Mauro's world map is oriented in Arabic fashion, with south at the top. And, the circular format and detailed cities are similar to mappaemundi.

In 1492, Italian explorer Christopher Columbus sailed west to reach Asia. Because of Ptolemy's map, he thought it would not be far. In fact, when he discovered several islands in the Caribbean Sea, he thought he had reached India. Columbus had no idea there were two great continents in his way.

Exploration continued to interest Europeans. In 1497, Italian navigator John Cabot explored the coasts of North America. That same year, Portuguese explorer Vasco da Gama followed

Vasco da Gama's voyage to India was a major accomplishment. It opened the first all-water trade route between Europe and Asia.

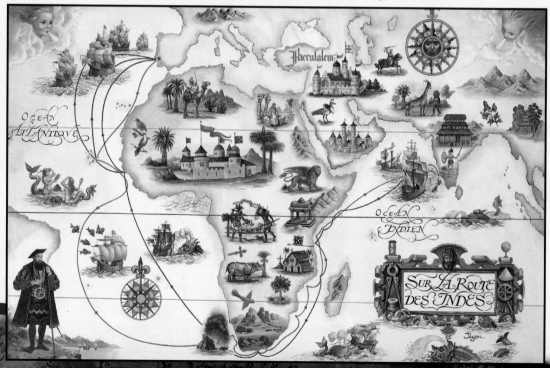

Dias's route around Africa to find his way to India. A new passage to Asia had finally been discovered!

Then in 1499, Italian navigator Amerigo Vespucci (vay-SPOOT-chee) began exploring along the coasts of South America. He was the first to realize that Columbus had not just found a couple of islands. An entire **New World** had been discovered!

Many European ships carried navigators. The navigators produced maps called portolan charts that had many directional lines marked on them. These charts were extremely valuable. They held the secrets of new lands and trade routes around the world.

First World Maps

When Waldseemüller created his map, North and South America had not yet been fully explored.

In 1507, German mapmaker Martin Waldseemüller (VAHLT-zay-mul-uhr) made the first map to include the name *America* for the **New World**. He named the new continents after Amerigo Vespucci. Waldseemüller's map featured the whole world east to west. But, it did not show the North and South poles.

The following year, Italian **cartographer** Francesco Rosselli made the first world map drawn with an oval **projection**. There were many errors, but the world was complete from pole to pole. His detailed map is only 6 by 11 inches (15 by 28 cm). Today, it is kept at the National Maritime Museum in Greenwich, England.

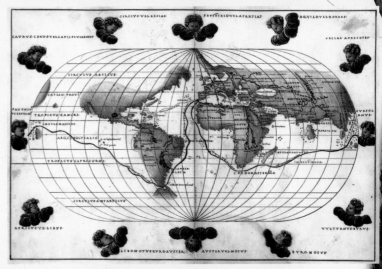

Ferdinand Magellan's route proved a ship could sail around the world.

These new world maps showed that a ship could sail west and end up where it began. So in 1519, navigator Ferdinand Magellan left Spain to sail around the world. He died on the voyage. But in 1522, one of his ships arrived back in Spain. Finally, there was no doubt about the shape of the earth and the lands upon it.

For centuries, people have tried to explain the world around them. The earliest sketches gradually developed into **accurate** maps of exploration and discovery. Today, maps help us understand where we are now and express where we want to go in the future.

FUN FACT

Until 1747, many cartographers believed California was an island! It was mapped this way for more than 100 years.

Charting

10,000 BC A carving on a mammoth tusk was made in Ukraine.

6200 BC A mural was painted on a wall in Turkey.

2500 BC Mesopotamians created a map on a clay tablet.

1150 BC The first geologic map was created on papyrus in Egypt.

500s BC Pythagoras lived in Greece, where he concluded the earth is a sphere.

300s BC Aristotle proved the earth is a sphere by observing a lunar eclipse.

200s BC Eratosthenes developed a grid system used to locate places on maps.

AD 23 Strabo wrote *Geography*.

150 Ptolemy wrote *Geographia* and created his famous world map that used coordinates.

800s Al-Khwarizmi improved the accuracy of Ptolemy's map.

995 Al-Biruni wrote *Cartography* and calculated the accurate distance around the earth.

the Course

1100s   Al-Idrisi traveled the world to create accurate maps.

1405–1435   Cheng Ho sailed to Africa, improving Chinese cartography.

1420–1460   Prince Henry the Navigator's crews explored and mapped the coast of Africa.

1457   Brother Mauro created a world map of Portuguese discoveries.

1488   Bartolomeu Dias was the first navigator to sail around the Cape of Good Hope.

1492   Christopher Columbus discovered the Caribbean.

1497   John Cabot explored the coasts of North America; Vasco da Gama discovered a route from Africa to India.

1499   Amerigo Vespucci realized Columbus's discovery was the New World.

1507   Martin Waldseemüller first put the name *America* on a map.

1508   Francesco Rosselli made the first complete world map.

1519–1522   Ferdinand Magellan's crew sailed around the world.

Glossary

accurate - free of errors.

cartographer - a maker of maps or charts.

coordinate - any of a set of numbers used to locate a point on a line or a surface.

fleet - a group of ships under one command.

geologic - relating to the science of Earth and its structure.

geometry - a branch of mathematics that deals with shapes, lines, and angles.

horizontal - in a side-to-side direction.

lunar eclipse - the total or partial cutting off of the light of the full moon by the earth's shadow. It occurs when the sun, the earth, and the moon are in, or almost in, a straight line.

Ming dynasty - the ruling Chinese dynasty from 1368 to 1644. A dynasty is a series of rulers who belong to the same family.

mural - a picture painted on a wall or a ceiling.

Muslim - a person who follows Islam. Islam is a religion based on the teachings of the prophet Muhammad as they appear in the Koran.

New World - another name for the Western Hemisphere, which
includes the continents of North America and South America.

projection - the representation, upon a flat surface, of all or part of
the surface of the earth or another celestial sphere.

sphere - a globe-shaped body.

vertical - in an up-and-down position.

Web Sites

To learn more about cartography visit ABDO Publishing Company
on the World Wide Web at **www.abdopublishing.com**. Web sites
about cartography are featured on our Book Links page. These links
are routinely monitored and updated to provide the most current
information available.

Index